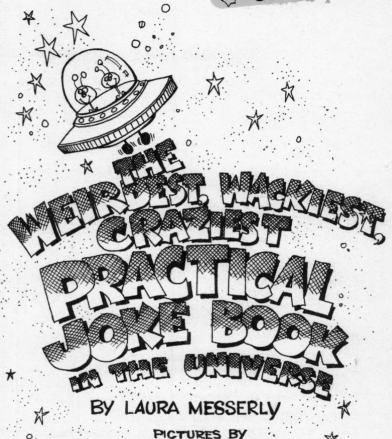

THE WEIRDEST, WACKIEST, CRAZIEST PRACTICAL JOKE BOOK IN THE UNIVERSE

BY LAURA MESSERLY

PICTURES BY
ROSE-ANN TISSERAND & GREG HUCULAK

Published by Willowisp Press, Inc.
401 E. Wilson Bridge Road, Worthington, Ohio 43085

Copyright©1990 by Willowisp Press, Inc.

Printed in the United States of America

10 9 8 7 6 5 4 3 2 1

ISBN 0-87406-444-9

CONTENTS

Introduction

It's happened to you before, hasn't it? Friends who think they're pretty smart pull a practical joke on you, leaving you all wet, or standing on your head, or just looking silly. Of course, since they're your friends, you're all really just having fun. Still, you'd like to be able to pull a fast one on them, too. . . all in fun, naturally!

Well, this book tells you how. There are loads of jokes here: knock-knock jokes that'll leave you groaning, brain teasers to stump the smartest, "impossible" tricks that you can really do, some simple magic tricks, and practical jokes that could start a war! None of the jokes need a lot of preparation, so you can do them almost anytime!

There's one important thing to remember, though. Jokes are supposed to be funny—both to you and the "victim." These jokes aren't for embarrassing someone you don't like. Instead it's probably best to play jokes only on people who will appreciate them. You'll have the most fun that way, anyway!

It's important to remember that when you're playing jokes, parents' and teachers' rules about safety and not making messes still apply. If you make a mess while playing a joke, be ready to clean it up afterward. If you're unsure about whether or not a joke is okay to do, it's a good idea to ask for permission before you try it. You have to think about what jokes would be right for birthday parties, or around the house, or at camp.

To get really good at playing jokes, you'll have to practice a lot. If you stumble on your words, it will be easy for people to see that they're in for it. Go over the jokes in your head before you try to tell them. Learn a smooth way of bringing up a riddle so that no one will even realize it's a joke until the punchline. Do your sleight-of-hand tricks by yourself or in front of a mirror a few times before you actually try to fool someone.

You can take these jokes and use them as they are, or change them yourself so they become your very own, original jokes. You might want to keep a pencil with you while you're reading this book. That way, you can write down your own ideas in the margins. Some day maybe you can even create your own joke book!

Knock-Knock 'Til You Drop!

Here are some knock-knock jokes that'll really "knock" your socks off, "knock" you out, "knock" you over—or maybe just give you the giggles!

Knock-knock!
Who's there?
Lettuce.
Lettuce who?
Lettuce in and you'll see!

Knock-knock!
Who's there?
I'm Mona Lisa.
I'm Mona Lisa who?
I'm Mona Lisa your house—I'm a real estate
agent.

Knock-knock!
Who's there?
Socks.
Socks who?
Socks you! [Punch person lightly in the arm.]

Knock-knock!
Who's there?
Yah.
Yah who?
I didn't know you were a cowboy.

Knock-knock!
Who's there?
Banana.
Banana who?
Knock-knock!
Who's there?
Banana.
Banana who?
Knock-knock!
Who's there?
Banana.
Banana who?
Knock-knock!
Who's there?
Orange.
Orange who?
Orange you glad I didn't say, "banana?"

Knock-knock!
Who's there?
Cows say.
Cows say who?
No, cows say, "Moo."

Knock-knock!
Who's there?
Atch.
Atch who?
Gesundheit!

Knock-knock!
Who's there?
Old lady.
Old lady who?
I didn't know you could yodel!

Knock-knock!
Who's there?
Howie.
Howie who?
I'm fine. Howie you?

Will you remember me even if we're not in the same class next year?

Sure.

Will you remember me if we're not in the same class till graduation?

Yes.

Will you always remember me?

Of course.

[Pause here for a minute or two. Then . . .]

Knock-knock!

Who's there?

I thought you said you'd always remember me!?!

Rib-Tickling Riddles

Question: What is silly, puzzling, and a little corny? *Answer:* The bunch of riddles you're about to read!

How do you divide 11 apples among 12 people?
Make applesauce.

What has a head, four legs, and a foot, but can't think or walk?
A bed.

What has four legs and leaves?
A table.

What has four legs and leaves?
A dog, after you yell at it.

What has four legs, two arms, and a back, but can't move?
A chair.

What has a tongue but can't talk?
A shoe.

What has eyes but can't see?
A potato.

What's blue and has two legs, but can't walk?
A pair of jeans.

What always has drawers?
Everybody. You don't go around without yours, do you?

What has eyes but can't see, ears but can't hear, legs but can't walk, and can jump as high as Mount Everest?
A dead horse. (Mount Everest can't jump, either.)

You Fell For It!

Here are some tricks that are sort of like riddles, a little bit like insults, and just plain daffy all the way around!

Do you want to hear a dirty joke?
Sure!
A white horse fell in the mud. Do you want to hear a clean joke?
Yeah.
A pig took a bath.

Did you hear the one about the broken record?
No.
Did you hear the one about the broken record?
I said, no.
Did you hear the one about the broken record?

Add these up: A ton of granite, two tons of cobwebs, three tons of fat, and four tons of miscellaneous rocks.... Do you have all that in your head?
Yes.
You sure do!

Think of any animal that lives in Africa.
Okay.
Now, close your eyes.
(Your friend closes his eyes.)
Dark, isn't it?

A friend of mine got snew in his computer.
What's snew?
Not much. What's new with you?

Pete and Repeat went for a walk in the woods. They swam through a river. They outran a bear. Then they came to a cave. Pete and Repeat went in. Pete got lost. Who was left?

Repeat.

Okay—you must not have understood it the first time. Pete and Repeat went for a walk...

Tongue Bunglers

Test your friends with a few tongue twisters. Here are some for starters. Do you know any more? It might be fun to try to make up some of your own, too!

* Sally sells seashells by the seashore.
* The sinking ship's seamen sadly sighed.
* Bad Bob bought a big bat.
* Armored Arnold always argues.
* Work book.
* Rubber baby buggy bumper.
* Sapsuckers suck sap.

Brain Busters

You can test your friends' brainpower with these baffling word problems. But *you'll* have to figure them out first!

Three men wanted to cross a river from Abbottsville to Barstead. Two of them weighed 100 pounds each, and the other weighed 300 pounds. The only boat around held just 300 pounds at a time. How did they all get across?

The answer: First, the two 100-pound men went across to Barstead. One stayed there while the other went back across to Abbottsville. The 300-pound man then crossed to Barstead by himself. When he got there, he got out, and the 100-pound man got back in the boat and went back to pick up the other 100-pound man at Abbottsville.

Ms. Johnson was on a business trip to Chicago, where she had never been before. While walking down the street, she ran into an old friend she hadn't seen or heard from in 10 years. With the friend was a little boy. "Hello," said the friend. "It's good to see you. Since I saw you last I got married. This is my little boy."

"What's your name?" Ms. Johnson asked the little boy.

"The same as my father's," he answered.

"Then your name is Tom," said Ms. Johnson. How did she know his name?

The friend she ran into was a man, whose name was Tom.

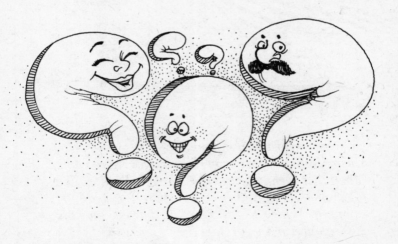

A dancer's sister died. But the woman who died had no sisters. How was this possible?

The dancer was a man.

Which is heavier, a pound of wood or a pound of feathers?

They're both a pound, of course.

Which is heavier, a pound of wood or a pound of gold?

In this case a pound of wood is heavier. Gold and other precious metals are weighed by a different standard than other things.

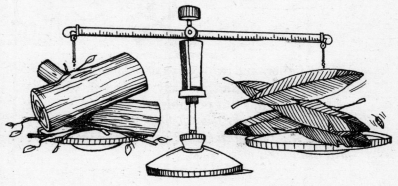

A big elephant and a little elephant were performing in the center ring of a circus. The little elephant was the big elephant's daughter, but the big elephant was not the little elephant's mother. How was this possible?

The big elephant was the little elephant's father.

Two fathers and two sons went fishing. Each of them caught a fish, but only three fish were caught. How was this possible?

Only three people went fishing. A grandfather and his son and grandson. The grandfather and grandson both were sons.

You are in a tent at camp. You have no flashlight. In your bag are three pairs of blue socks and three pairs of black socks.

You want to put on a matched pair. You're going to take some socks out by the fire where you can see to put them on.

What is the least number of socks you have to take from your bag to be sure you have at least one matched pair?

Three. (Think about it for a moment. No matter what color the three socks you pull out are, you're sure to have either two blue ones or two black ones.)

A coin dealer tries to sell you a coin from the Roman empire. The coin is dated 75 B.C. How do you know he's a dishonest salesman?

Stop and think. People in those times would have no way of knowing they were in B.C. years.

Three men were in a boat in the middle of the ocean. The boat turned over, but only two of them got their hair wet. Why?

One of them was bald.

A farmer had 19 pigs. All but nine died. How many pigs did the farmer have left?

The answer, of course, is nine. But most people will subtract the nine instead, and answer 10.

My father has a son and no daughters. The son is not my brother. Who is he?

Me!

I have two coins in my hand that add up to fifteen cents, and one of them isn't a nickel. What am I holding?

A dime and a nickel. (The dime is the one that isn't a nickel!)

There are six children walking down the street. You want to give them a bag of six cookies. How do you give each child a cookie and still leave one in the bag?

Give five of them one cookie each from the bag. Give the sixth a cookie that is still in the bag.

A girl dreamed she and her two friends were in a burning building. She saw a way to escape, but she could only save one of her friends. The fire was coming closer and closer. What should she do?

Wake up.

John and Martha were lying on the floor in a puddle of water and broken glass. They were dead. A cat sat on a table nearby. What happened?

John and Martha were fish. The cat knocked their bowl off the table.

A man was found dead in a room with 53 bicycles. When the police looked at the room, they knew immediately someone had killed him for cheating at cards. How did they figure it out?

It was the 53 bicycles. The man had been playing cards with "Bicycle" brand playing cards. Normally there are only 52 cards in a deck. Since there were 53 cards in the room, the murdered man must have been holding extra cards.

A man went to the pet store and bought a parrot. The salesman said the bird would repeat everything it heard. The man took the bird home and kept it for two weeks. The bird never said a word. The man took the bird back to the store and complained that the salesman had lied to him. But the salesman insisted he had told the truth. How could he have?

The parrot was deaf.

One morning a bank's night watchman came running up to the bank president and said, "Last night, I had a terrible dream that the bank was going to be robbed today. I'm sure it will come true! What are you going to do?"

The bank president took immediate action—he fired the worried watchman. Why?

The watchman had been sleeping on the job.

Tricky Tricks

Tricky tricks are sneaky little jokes that you can play on friends or relatives. You might get a million laughs—or maybe a million tomatoes thrown at you!

Too close for comfort. On a little piece of paper, write in tiny letters, If you can read this you are too close! Pin it to your shirt and see how many people come up and try to read it.

Confetti fun. The next time you write a friend a letter, try putting confetti in the folds of the paper before you put it in the envelope. When she opens the letter, the confetti will spill out all over her!

Instead of confetti, you could also try using glitter, potpourri, or lawn clippings.

Hot spot. A gag everyone's probably fallen for time and again is the old "What's that spot on your shirt?" trick.

Just point and look at your friend's shirt as if there were something on it. When he looks down to see what's there, lift your hand and flip his nose lightly with your knuckle. Or just say something like, "Made you look!" to let him know you've pulled one over on him.

There are many ways to do this trick. You could just point up in the sky or down the street to fool your friend. Or look down at the ground and say, "Your shoelaces are untied." Even a person wearing shoes with no laces will look!

Tear 'em up. Tell your friends that if they each can tear a piece of paper into four equal pieces, you'll give each of them a quarter. When they do it, hand each of them one of the torn pieces of paper and say, "Here's your quarter!" (It's a quarter of the paper.)

All-expense-paid trip to...nowhere! A fake letter can be a funny joke to play on a friend. Pretend you're from a radio station or a department store, and write a letter to your friend saying he has won a prize.

Type the letter, or ask an older brother or sister to type it, so that it looks official. Say in the letter that you'll be sending a secret prize soon.

After your friend gets the letter and tells everyone he's won a prize, send him another letter. Fill it with confetti, and tell him it was all a joke. You can write something like "SURPRISE! You didn't win a prize after all! From your sneaky friend." Or maybe try a rhyme:

There once was a kid in this town,
Who thought he was really a clown.
He wrote his friends notes,
That turned out to be jokes—
To give them all smiles, not frowns.

Look! Up in the sky! It's a bird, it's a plane, it's...nothing. One of the best "made-you-look" jokes is the school cafeteria version. You can fool lots of people at one time, too. It works best if you get some kids you eat lunch with in on it. Try to get a table under an air-conditioning vent. During lunch, look up at the vent for a few seconds. Then, get everyone at your table to look up at the vent. Just keep looking and pointing, and in a little while you'll see that people all over the cafeteria are beginning to wonder what you're looking at. Now, you and your friends know there's nothing up there, but pretty soon, students and teachers will be coming by trying to see what's so interesting in the air-conditioning vent. But the joke will be on them!

Honesty test. For this trick you will need an empty billfold, a spool of dark thread, and a passerby. (It can be someone you know.) Tie the thread through the fold of the billfold and put it down on the ground as if someone had dropped it. It's best to put it on grass, where the thread will be harder to see. Take the spool and let out the thread until you can hide behind a bush or the corner of a house. But be sure you can keep an eye on the billfold.

When someone comes along and leans down to pick the billfold up, pull it out of their reach with the thread. See how long it takes them to find you! (For even more fun, take some fake money from a board game in your house and put it in the wallet to fatten it up. You could even let a little of it stick out.)

Amazing ghost arm. Tell your friend you have a ghost at your house. The ghost will show his presence by lifting up your friend's arm. Have your friend stand with his side near a wall. Tell him to press against the wall with the back of his hand while he whispers some secret words you have told him to say. He should say them over and over till you tell him the ghost is near.

Pretend to concentrate on the ghost, but actually count to 60 while your friend is pushing against the wall. When you get to 60, tell your friend to stop chanting. Next, tell him to stand in the center of the room, close his eyes, and relax completely. A few seconds later, he will feel his arm begin to rise as if by magic.

(There is no real ghost here, of course. Your friend's arm muscles are just reacting to the way he pressed against the wall.)

Along came a spider... This is a trick that works best in the dark. Try it at camp or at a slumber party or when you have a friend spending the night. You'll need a spool of dark thread and some masking tape. Cut a piece of the tape wide enough to go across a doorway. Then lay the piece of tape on a table with the sticky side up. Cut lots of pieces of thread about a yard long each, and then stick one end of each thread to the tape. Last, put the tape above a doorway. When someone walks through the doorway, it'll feel like he is walking into spider webs!

Family Funnies

Here are some pranks that you can play on any member of your family. But remember, go easy on Mom and Dad if you have an allowance at stake!

A fortune in laughs. If your family likes to have Chinese food for dinner sometimes, complete with fortune cookies, you've got a chance to set up a good joke.

Before dinner, write up some funny fortunes on tiny slips of paper and use them to replace the fortunes that came in the cookies. (You might have to use tweezers [wash them first] to get the fortunes in and out.) You can make up silly fortunes, such as, "You will soon meet a stranger who is stranger than you are!" Better yet, make one of the fortunes a warning to someone that a practical joke will soon be played on him.

Brotherly blockout. These are two good tricks to try on an older brother or sister. After the person has gone to bed, use masking tape to fasten newspaper or cut-open grocery bags over his entire door opening. When he opens his door in the morning, he'll have to get through a wall of paper.

Or, just fasten strips of masking tape from the top to the bottom of the door frame all the way across it. The best part about this joke is that the tape slows down your victim—who will no doubt be chasing you!

Checker-decker. Place a red checker on a table. Then bet your mom or dad an extra portion of tonight's dessert that they can't put a black checker under the red one without touching it with their fingers or anything else. They'll think for a while, but won't be able to figure it out.

Then, just hold the black checker underneath the table right under the red one. You win!

Pleasant dreams. Take some books and put them under your brother or sister's pillow inside the pillowcase. They probably won't notice the books until they plop their heads down on the hard surface.

Putting something unexpected under the covers at the foot of the bed is funny, too. Try putting a prickly hairbrush in your sister's bed. Just be sure you don't put something so big in the bed that the person can see that something's there before he puts his feet under the covers.

Eggs-actly perfect predicament. For this trick you'll need a raw egg and a door that will stand ajar (that is, not swing shut and pinch a person's fingers). There must be just enough space between the hinges for a hand to slip through.

Tell your friend, or gullible little brother, that you can show him how to pull an egg through the crack between a door' hinges. Have him slip his hand—or just his thumb and forefinger if his hands are too large—through the crack. Next, put the egg in his hand.

All you have to do is walk away, and the trick will be complete! He can't reach the egg with his other hand because of the door. And if he drops the egg, he'll make a big mess. He'll just have to wait for someone to come along and help him out!

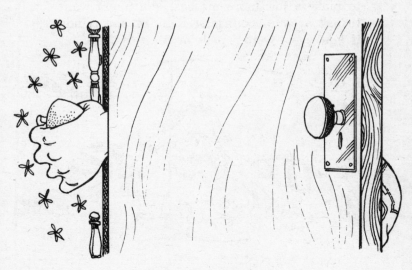

Heart-stopping pillow propping. This is one of the oldest and funniest tricks around.

Before a person enters a room, prop a pillow on the top of the door and tilt it against the top of the door frame. Then, when he pushes the door open to walk through, the pillow will plop right on top of his head.

A good time to play this prank is when the person is going to bed. The room he's entering will be dark, and he'll be tired, so he probably won't see the pillow above the door.

Here's another version of this trick that's really fun if you're away at camp. Instead of putting a pillow above the door, use a water balloon! (A water balloon at home could get you into trouble with your parents. But when you're in a cabin at camp, it's probably okay to make a few more messes. You might want to ask a camp counselor if he or she minds if you use a water balloon for this trick.)

It's not easy eating green. Put a couple drops of green food coloring into the applesauce your family was supposed to eat for dinner. Everyone will think it's spoiled until you prove you're brave enough to eat some. Can you think of any other foods to color?

Drawers on the floors. A fun and easy trick is to turn someone's desk or dresser drawers upside down and put them back in.

When the person opens the drawers again, everything inside will fall on the floor. This works best with a drawer of papers or clothes instead of little items. Big items can be held in place with your hand long enough to set up the trick.

Just be sure that nothing in the drawer is breakable. You don't want to damage someone's property.

This trick works especially well if the furniture has layers between the drawers instead of open space. (To see what we mean, take out the top drawer of a dresser. If you can't see into the next drawer down, you've got a good dresser for this trick.)

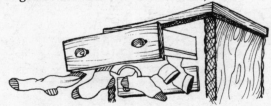

Just switching someone's drawers around is a good trick, too. The person won't know where to find anything!

Or, take everything out of somebody's drawers and hide it all someplace. You could hide the stuff in the closet, or maybe in a place where the person won't look right away.

Slip-slidin' away. This classic trick is very simple. All you have to do is lightly coat someone's doorknob with petroleum jelly. She'll try to open the door, but she won't be able to open it without cleaning it first.

Wouldn't it be fun to watch her try to figure it out? If you decide to stay on the same side of the door with her, be sure she doesn't know you're the one who pulled the trick!

An alarming experience! If someone in your family has a radio alarm clock, a quick and easy prank is simply to turn up the volume. When the alarm goes off, that person will *really* jump out of bed!

Hearing bells. This will really wake mom and dad up in a hurry! After they go to sleep with their alarm clock set, hide it somewhere in the room. They'll be able to hear the alarm when it goes off, but when mom or dad reaches to shut it off, it won't be there. They'll be in a real panic if they can't find it right away!

This is your wake-up call. Set someone's alarm clock to go off on a morning when he had planned to sleep in. But be sure it's someone you can outrun!

For another twist, set someone's alarm half an hour early (not late, though, you don't want to make anyone late for school or work).

Salad with your toothpaste? Flavor your family's toothbrushes by soaking the brush ends in vinegar for a while. The next time they brush their teeth, they'll be surprised at the awful taste of their usual toothpaste!

Light as a brick? Substitute a heavy item for something that's normally light, or vice versa. For instance, you could put a brick in your sister's lunch bag in place of her food one morning. It won't take her long to realize you've pulled one over on her. Or, take the heavy football padding out of your brother's gym bag and stuff the bag with a pillow.

Magical Mayhem

You can amaze people with these easy magic tricks. The best part is that you don't need a top hat or a magic wand—just a few household items and some gullible friends!

Get the lead out! All you'll need for this trick is a nice long pencil and a clear glass about three-quarters full of water.

Show a friend the pencil before you start so he can see that it is not broken. Then, put the pencil in the glass and let it rest against the side. If your friend looks through the side of the glass, the pencil will look like it is broken. Next, take the pencil out of the water. Of course, it will still be whole.

Easy backward, too. Tell your friend you can teach him to see backward with that same glass of water.

Take a 3-by-5-inch index card and draw an arrow on it lengthwise. Hold it behind the glass of water, right next to the glass, and have your friend watch it. Mutter magic words as you move the card away from the glass slowly. The arrow will seem to reverse itself!

Floating finger. Show a friend how you can make a magic finger appear between his two index fingers.

Have him hold his two index fingers tip-to-tip several inches in front of his eyes. If he looks past them at the wall, a little finger, with a nail on each end, will appear between the tips of his fingers. If he pulls his fingers apart a little bit, the magic finger will float in midair.

A tight squeeze. Tell your friend you can magically put him or her right through the spokes of your bicycle. Your friend probably won't believe you. Then, whip out a piece of paper and a pencil. Write "him" or "her" on the paper and put it through the bicycle spokes!

You could also tell people "I'm going to put myself through this knothole in the fence" or through a curtain ring or other small opening. Then write "myself" on a piece of paper and do your trick. How many other new ways can you think of to play this joke?

What a joker. After that "tight squeeze" trick, tell your friend you can walk through a playing card or other small piece of paper. He'll know something's up, especially after that last joke, but he'll want to see how you'll do it this time. Take the card (use the rules card or joker, so you won't ruin your deck), and fold it in half lengthwise. Now cut slits in it, as in the illustration.

When you open the card up and stretch it out, you really will be able to step right through the playing card!

Pushy, pushy. The next time you and a friend are studying together and take a break, tell him you're so strong you can push one of your textbooks right through a circle made by touching your thumb and forefinger.

Set the book on the table. With one hand, make the circle. Hold the circle near the book. Put a finger from the other hand through the circle and push the book across the table.

Hocus-pocus. Have you ever seen a magician pull a tablecloth off a table, leaving all the dishes standing in place? You can do the same sort of thing without breaking a lot of dishes practicing!

All you'll need for this trick is a playing card or 3-by-5-inch index card and a quarter. (You'll probably need to practice this trick for a while before you show anyone.) Hold your forefinger out, curling your other fingers back into a fist. Balance the card on your finger, and put the quarter on top of that.

Ask a friend to remove the card but leave the quarter where it is—without touching the quarter! Chances are, your friend won't be able to do it. You can show him how to do the trick: Flick the edge of the card quickly with the fingers of your other hand. The card will fly away, and the coin will stay in place.

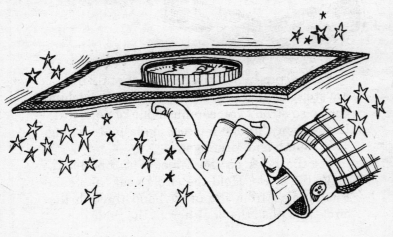

Ten sense. For this trick, you'll need an empty, narrow-neck bottle, a dime, a toothpick or a wooden match, and some water.

Bend the toothpick in half till it snaps and forms a V. But don't break it completely; leave the halves attached by thin bits of wood. Put the bent toothpick across the top of the bottle. Lay the dime on top of the toothpick. Tell your friend you can get the dime into the bottle without touching the bottle, the dime, or the toothpick.

When he tells you that's impossible, all you have to do is drop some of the water from a spoon or your finger onto the corner of the toothpick. This will make the toothpick straighten, and the dime will drop into the bottle.

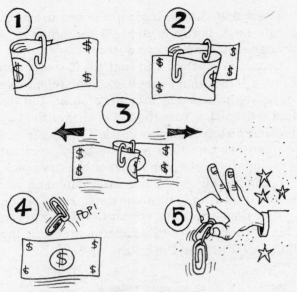

Magnetic magic. Bring out two "special" paper clips you keep in a "special" box. Tell your friends that these may look like regular paper clips, but they are really magic clips. They are trained to link together on command.

Next, bring out a dollar bill or a piece of paper that is about the same size as a dollar. Fold the paper in an *S* shape, and put the paper clips on it as you see here.

Then grab the paper by each end and say, "Now, magic clips!" Quickly pull the ends of the paper out straight.

The clips will jump into the air, and when they land, they will be joined!

A knotty problem. Take a piece of string or yarn about two feet long and lay it out straight on a table. Ask someone to hold it by its two ends, and, without letting go of either end, tie the string in a knot. Can't be done, right?

Well, it's easy when you know how! All you need to do is fold your arms first, grab one end of the string in each hand, and unfold your arms. (When you fold your arms, be sure that one hand comes out in front of your arms and the other is behind your arms next to your chest.) The knot will be tied automatically.

Mind-reading. With this trick you can read the thoughts of a whole roomful of people! You can, that is, if you have a sneaky partner who is in on your joke.

Have your friends sit in a circle. Tell them that after you leave the room they should decide on a number between one and 10. When you return, ask them all to concentrate on this number. You must go up to all of the people and put your hands on their temples to try to read their thought waves. This is where your secret partner comes in. When you touch his temples, he should clench his teeth as many times as the chosen number. You'll be able to feel this with your fingers. After you've felt everyone's temples, announce the secret number! No one will guess how you did it.

The secret number. For this trick you'll need a piece of paper and a pencil, a box or bowl, and an audience of at least one.

Fold the paper in thirds in one direction, unfold it, and fold it in thirds in the other direction. Flatten the paper again; it should look like a tic-tac-toe board. Tear the paper along those fold lines.

Give the pencil to the person you're fooling. You will give him all the pieces of paper and ask him to write something on each one without letting you see it. He can write numbers, or names, or animals, or whatever he chooses.

When you give him the paper, however, secretly give him the middle piece first.

After he writes on each paper, he should put it in the box.

Now, ask your friend to concentrate on the first thing he wrote. You, with your eyes closed, will be able to pick out the piece of paper he is concentrating on. How? It will be the only piece of paper in the bowl that has torn edges on all sides.

Everyone will be amazed to see you choose and read the correct piece of paper.

Betcha Can't!

Betcha can'ts are tricks that you know *can* be done. But since they seem so impossible, your friends will betcha can't!

Trapped! This trick requires a plastic bowl half full of water, and a mop or stick of some kind.

Bet your friend that he can't hold the bowl of water against the ceiling with a mop handle for 15 seconds. As most friends usually do, he'll take the bet.

Get on a step stool and put the bowl against the ceiling. Have your friend put the handle against the bottom of the bowl. When he's got the handle in the right place to hold the bowl, get down from the stool and put it out of your friend's reach. Now, tell him you forgot your watch and leave the room to get it—but don't come back!

When your friend has won the bet, he'll be unable to collect from you, because he's been trapped into holding a bowl of water against the ceiling. He'll just have to stay there until help comes along!

It's probably best to do this trick in a garage, just in case the water spills.

For book-lovers. Tell your friend you'll show him how you can touch a book outside and inside without opening it. He'll say you're wrong. Here's how to prove yourself right. Pick up the book and walk outside. Say, "Now, I'm touching the book outside." Then go back inside and say, "Now, I'm touching the book inside."

You can work this trick with a box or a jar, too. Try to think up other ways to make this trick your own creation.

Double your money. Bet your friend a quarter that you can magically double his money. Get a clear glass and center a quarter in the bottom of the glass. Now, slowly pour about an inch of water into the glass. (Be sure not to move the quarter when you do this.)

Tell your friend to look at the glass from the side, just above the water level. He will see what looks like two coins. One coin will be at the bottom, and another will appear to be floating on top of the water.

X-ray vision. Make a bet with your friend that you can put a hole in her hand without her feeling it. Or, just tell her you have X-ray vision, and can give it to her, too. All you'll need for this trick is the cardboard tube from waxed paper or paper towels. Or, make your own tube out of paper about the same size.

Have your friend close her eyes. Put the tube in her left hand and have her put it up to her left eye. Then have her put her right hand, palm toward her, against the side of the tube near the end. Now, have her open her eyes and focus on something across the room. She will seem to be able to see the room through a hole that has appeared in her hand.

You could make this a magic trick by using magic words and decorating the tube with stars.

Barrier bet. You'll need at least two friends to play this joke on, plus a kitchen rug or newspaper.

Bet your friends you can have them both stand on the same rug or newspaper, yet be unable to touch each other. Of course, they'll take the bet.

Here's the easy way to win: Place the rug or paper across a doorway. Have one friend stand on the rug in one room, shut the door and have the other friend stand on it in the other room. Now they are both on the same rug, but a door separates them.

(Hint: If this is ever played on you, try touching the other person's fingers under the door.)

Which finger? This is sort of a coordination test, but you can turn it into a bet that few people will win. Here's how it works: Have your subject hold his arms out with his palms facing outward. Then have him cross one arm over the other so his palms face each other. Make him clasp his hands and interlock his fingers. Then have him bring his hands down, bend his elbows and bring his hands up through his arms past his chest. (And this isn't even the test part!)

Now, the test: Point to any one of your subject's fingers (*don't* touch the finger) and ask him to wiggle it. Most people will move the same finger on the other hand.

(Hint: Try not to let the person stop and concentrate for too long on which finger you're pointing at. Most people don't anyway, because this trick looks so simple.)

Out of line. Line up some coins—let's say six or eight nickels—on a desktop. They should be in a perfectly straight line and touching each other.

Bet your friend that he can't make the last nickel in the line move away from the rest without touching it. He might try blowing it, but that probably won't work. Here's what you do: Put your finger on the *first* nickel in the line. Slide it back from the others, then quickly slide it back against nickel number two. Hitting that end of the line will bump the last coin away from the group.

Did you ever hear in your science class that for every action there is a reaction? This is a good example of that. But you should remember that if your action against your subject is really sneaky, look out for his *reaction!*

In a clinch. Most everybody falls for this old joke.

Tell your friend you can make him clasp his hands in such a way that he won't be able to leave the house without letting them go. (This trick works especially well on big, strong, older brothers.)

Unless you've been playing too many tricks on this friend, he's sure to take you up on it. All you have to do is find a heavy piece of furniture—like a piano or a staircase railing. Have your friend put his arms around the piano leg or through the railing and clasp his hands. Until he lets go, he'll be stuck where he is.

Camp Cutups and
Party Pranks

These pranks are great to play at camp or at parties, when you'll have a bunch of people around to enjoy them! They're a little harder to pull off, but they're guaranteed to get laughs!

Clouds rolling in. For this trick you'll need some talcum powder and a blow dryer. It works best on hardwood or linoleum floors. You'd have a hard time doing it on carpet. If your roommates at camp take too long in the bathroom, this prank will get them out quickly.

When they're in the bathroom, sprinkle powder just in front of the door. Then, turn the dryer on low and blow it under the door. The cloud of powder coming out on the other side of the door will get your friends out of the bathroom in a hurry!

This trick can be even more fun if you play it anonymously. When one of your campmates' rooms is empty, sneak down the hall and blow some powder into his room. He'll be in for quite a surprise when he gets back!

Smooth and creamy. This prank is good for camp, too. You'll need shaving cream and a paper bag or an old, unused record album cover for this trick.

Fill the bag or cardboard cover with shaving cream. Slip the open end under the door of an unsuspecting person and quickly stomp on the bag and run away! The shaving cream will squirt all over the floor on the other side of the door.

Another slippery trick. This one is a favorite at summer camp, where rules are usually pretty relaxed. Remember the petroleum jelly you used to keep someone from opening a door? Now use it to lightly coat a toilet seat.

The next person who tries to sit down on the seat is in for a slippery, sticky surprise!

Ick! This camp prank can be messy. (Remember this before you play it. You may have to clean it up!) You know those packets of mustard and ketchup you get at fast food restaurants? If you just barely open a corner of one, and put it under a toilet seat where the little knobs rest on the rim of the bowl, the person who sits down next may get squirted (or may squirt the floor, depending on which way you face the opening end).

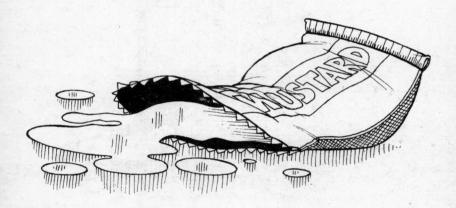

John the Baptist. Here's another good camp trick! When your friend is in the bathroom stall, get a big glass of cold water. Go to the stall and knock on the door. When he asks, "Who is it?" say, "John the Baptist!" and throw the cold water over the door onto him.

Snipe snooping. You can come up with many variations of this famous old joke. It's often used as an initiation prank for a club or by a group of campers. It's called snipe hunting.

Here's the story line: A group of jokesters tells a person that they are going out on a snipe hunt that night. "If you promise to do as we tell you, you can come along with us," they say. To the unsuspecting person, snipe hunting sounds like it must be lots of fun.

The hunters give the victim a bag to catch the snipes in. They tell him to wait behind a bush with the bag until the snipes go running by. The hunters then go off, saying they'll chase the snipes back toward the bag man so that he can catch the snipes more quickly.

But what they really do is go back to the campsite or clubhouse, have a soda pop and some potato chips, and laugh about someone silly enough to sit behind a bush with a bag and wait for snipes.

Then, they go out and bring the person back so he can join in on the fun. They tell the victim that there is no such thing as a snipe, and that the joke

Two hints: Lots of people who have never been on a snipe hunt have heard of it. You might try making up a new name for snipe hunting. Also, it helps to make up a good description of a "snipe" to convince the person that snipes are real animals.

All wet. When your friend at camp (or a family member at home) is taking a shower, slip quietly into the bathroom and remove all the towels.

Short sheeting. Here's another good prank for camp, or for an older brother or sister who thinks he or she is too smart to fall for your jokes.

During the day, go to your victim's bed and take off the covers and pillows. Now, loosen the top sheet at the foot of the bed. Pull the top sheet up and tuck the top edge of that sheet in at the head of the bed as if it were the fitted sheet. Now bring up the part of the sheet that had been tucked in at the foot, folding the sheet in half about midway down the bed. Put this part at the top of the bed like a normal top sheet. Now put the pillows and covers back on the bed.

If you've done this right, here's what will happen: Your victim will pull back the covers and climb into bed, but, because the top sheet is folded back on itself, the person will only be able to get halfway down the bed.

Now you see it. This is an easy one that is
sure to get lots of groans. At a party, bet your
friends that you can put a spoon (or a pencil or a
coin, or some other handy, small item) on a table,
put a box over it, and then remove the item from
the table without touching the box. Most everyone will bet that you can't do it.

Ask everybody to be quiet so that you can
concentrate. Put the item on the table, and put
the box over it. (Be sure the box sits evenly on the
table so that no one can see under it.)

Now say some magic words and wave your
hands over the box. Shut your eyes and pretend
to concentrate. Then, suddenly open your eyes
and announce that the item has disappeared. No
one will believe you, naturally, without checking
under the box. Someone who doesn't believe you
will lift the box and say, "There it is!" That is just
the time for you to pick up the item and say, "Now
I have removed it without touching the box!"

Blind man's bluff. This prank is great for parties.

You'll need to let others in on your trick. Set up an obstacle course of pillows, books, a wastebasket, or other small items on your living room floor. Choose one person who doesn't know the trick to go through the course blindfolded. Before he does, however, let him see and memorize the course. Let him count off how many steps there are between the items.

Now, blindfold him. While you do, be sure to talk a lot about what he's going to do, how difficult it will be, etc. While you are distracting him with talk, have others *remove* all of the obstacles. Then start him on his course.

Everyone will get a big kick out of seeing him wind his way carefully and thoughtfully across an empty floor.

Magic balloon. Next time you're giving a party with balloon decorations, try this trick. Put a

piece of clear tape an inch or so long on one or two of the balloons.

As a party trick, tell your guests you can put a magic spell on balloons so that if you stick pins in them, they won't burst. To demonstrate, burst a balloon by sticking a pin into it. Then, say magic words over one of the taped balloons (no one will be able to see the tape). Stick a pin through the tape, and the balloon will not burst.

Performance hint: If you put a small piece of tape on every balloon, you can let your guests choose the balloons you will jab with a pin. Then your trick will look even more realistic.

Slumber party tradition. At a slumber party it's traditional to pull a trick on the first person who falls asleep. One favorite is to put ice down the back of the first sleeper.

Another old trick is to put the sleeping person's hand in a bowl of lukewarm water—it's said to make the person wet the bed.

Good things in small packages. Here's a great birthday party trick. If you're giving a friend a small gift, put it in the right size box, but put that box in a larger one, and that one in a larger one, etc. You can wrap only the largest box, or all of them, if you like.

You might end up giving your friend earrings or a deck of cards in a refrigerator box! Won't everyone be surprised!

Splat! The next time you put up balloons for a party, try putting a little water in some of them before you blow them up. Then, if people pop some for fun, they'll get more than they bargained for.

Don't move a muscle. Make a bet with your classmate that there's a place in the room you could have him stand where he won't be able to lift his right foot off the floor. Assure him he will be standing with both feet flat on the floor, and you will not hold him down or put anything on him.

Next, have him stand so that his left shoulder, hip, and foot are against a wall. Try as he might, he won't be able to lift that right foot from the floor without falling over.

Repeat after me. This is a good trick for late at night at a slumber party, when everyone is getting a little punchy and will laugh at just about anything.

Convince your fellow partiers that you know magic words that will put them all in a trance. Have them repeat slowly after you, "Owa, tagoo, fiam. Owa, tagoo, fiam." They should all say it over and over faster and faster.

Pretty soon they'll realize they're saying, "Oh, what a goof I am!"

Gross-outs. These ideas would be good for a game of truth or dare or for a club initiation. They require a blindfolded person. Everyone should gather around while the blindfolded person puts his hand into a bowl of:

    —eyeballs (peeled grapes)
    —*jumbo* eyeballs (peeled hard-boiled eggs)
    —worms (cold, cooked spaghetti)
    —chopped brains (cut-up gelatin)

The final act of bravery would be for the person to put his hand into a bowl of the gross stuff and pick some out and eat it.

It helps the effect if you have the other people standing around make remarks like, "Ooh, look at those worms squirm!"